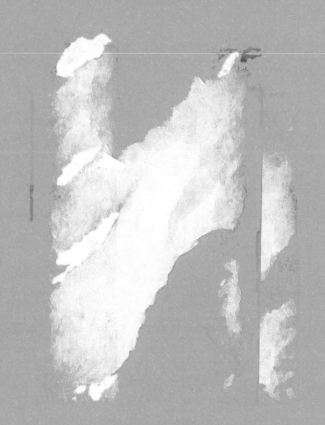

Recycle,
Reduce,
Reuse,
Rethink

Aluminum

Kate Walker

Smart Apple Media

Smart Apple Media
1980 Lookout Drive
North Mankato
Minnesota 56003

Library of Congress Cataloging-in-Publication Data

Walker, Kate.
  Aluminum / by Kate Walker.
  p. cm. — (Recycle, reduce, reuse, rethink)
  Includes index.
  ISBN 1-58340-559-3 (alk. paper)
  1. Aluminum industry and trade—Environmental aspects—Juvenile literature.
  2. Aluminum—Recycling—Juvenile literature. I. Title. II. Series.

TD195.A37W35 2004
669'.722'0286—dc22   2003070418

First Edition
9 8 7 6 5 4 3 2 1

First published in 2004 by
MACMILLAN EDUCATION AUSTRALIA PTY LTD
627 Chapel Street, South Yarra, Australia, 3141

Associated companies and representatives throughout the world.

Copyright © Kate Walker 2004

Edited by Helena Newton
Text and cover design by Cristina Neri, Canary Graphic Design
Technical illustrations and cartoons by Vaughan Duck
Photo research by Legend Images

Printed in China

Acknowledgements
The author and the publisher are grateful to the following for permission to reproduce copyright material:

Cover photograph: recycling aluminum cans, courtesy of Alcoa Australia.

Aberdeenshire Council, Housing & Social Work, p. 25; Alcoa Australia, p. 8; Jacques Jangoux/Auscape International, p. 11; Burnt Offerings Studio, p. 26; Centers for Disease Control and Prevention (U.S.A.), Public Health Image Library, p. 15; Coo-ee Picture Library, p. 16; Digital Vision, p. 5 (bottom); Getty Image/Brand X Pictures, p. 20; Getty News, p. 19; Sue & Graham Gooderham, p. 27; Great Southern Stock, pp. 9, 18; Imageaddict, p. 5 (top); Jiri Lochman/Lochman Transparencies, pp. 10, 12, 13; Mountstar Metal Corporation Ltd, p. 22 (both); Photodisc, pp. 5 (center), 21, 29 & design features; Gary Riches and the Oakville Scouts, p. 24; Savage & Chadwick Architects, Isle of Mann, p. 14; Terry Oakley/The Picture Source, p. 17; Tomra, p. 23.

While every care has been taken to trace and acknowledge copyright, the publisher tenders their apologies for any accidental infringement where copyright has proved untraceable. Where the attempt has been unsuccessful, the publisher welcomes information that would redress the situation.

Contents

Let's start recycling now!

Recycling **4**

What is aluminum? **5**

How aluminum is recycled **6**

Recycled aluminum products **8**

Why recycle aluminum? **10**

For and against recycling **16**

Reduce, reuse, rethink **18**

What governments are doing **20**

What industries are doing **22**

What communities are doing **24**

What individuals are doing **26**

What you can do **28**

Decomposition timeline **30**

Glossary **31**

Index **32**

When a word is printed in **bold**, you can look up its meaning in the glossary on page 31.

Recycling

Recycling means using products and materials again to make new products instead of throwing them away.

Why recycle?

Developed countries have become known as "throw-away societies" because they use and throw away so many products, often after just one use! Single-use products include drink cans, glass jars, sheets of paper, and plastic bags. Today, there are approximately six billion people in the world. By the year 2050, there could be as many as nine billion people. The world's population is growing fast, and people are using a lot more products and materials than they did in the past.

Instead of throwing products away, we can recycle them. When we recycle:

- ↻ we use fewer of the Earth's **natural resources**
- ↻ manufacturing is "greener" because recycling creates less **pollution** than using **raw materials**
- ↻ we reduce waste, which is better for the environment.

Governments, industries, communities, and individuals all around the world are finding different ways to solve the problems of how to conserve resources, reduce manufacturing pollution and waste, and protect the environment. If the Earth is to support nine billion people in the future, it is important that we all start recycling now!

As well as recycling, we can:

- ↻ reduce the number of products and materials we use
- ↻ reuse products and materials
- ↻ rethink the way we use products and materials.

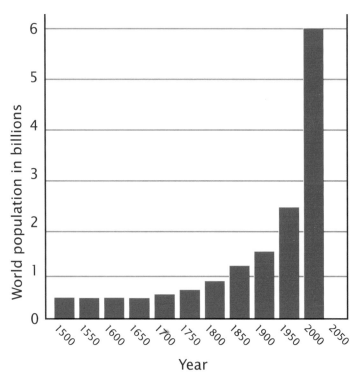

Today, there are more people on Earth using more products and materials than in the past, and the population is still growing.

What is aluminum?

Aluminum is a silver-white metal that is strong, lightweight, and easily bent into shape. Aluminum is never found in a pure form in nature. Rather, it is found as a red rock called **bauxite**. Bauxite is aluminum, oxygen, iron, and clay mixed together.

The history of aluminum

Aluminum was discovered in 1807 by Englishman Sir Humphry Davy. Davy found the new metal after pouring acid onto clay. This new metal, which he called **alumina**, was still bonded with oxygen, and he could not separate the two. About 70 years later, two men in different parts of the world discovered how to get pure aluminum from bauxite. They were Paul Heroult of France and Charles Martin Hall of the United States. They used other substances to dissolve alumina and then passed an electric current through it. The electricity drove off the oxygen and left pure aluminum behind.

Aluminum products today

Today, aluminum is used for:
- drink cans
- thin sheets of foil
- window and door frames
- outdoor furniture and railings
- car parts and engines
- aircraft bodies.

How aluminum is

Some aluminum is buried in **landfills** and some is recycled. The average household in a developed country throws away 18 pounds (8 kg) of aluminum each year.

The aluminum that is recycled goes through many processes.

1

People separate used aluminum foil and cans from other aluminum waste. Other aluminum waste is recycled at scrap metal yards. Only foil and cans are put out for curbside collection.

2 The aluminum foil and cans are collected by a truck and taken to the recycling center.

3 At the recycling center, aluminum is separated into two **pure streams** of foil and cans.

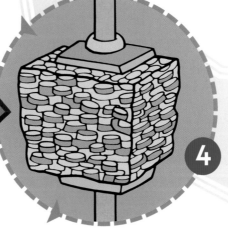

4 The pure-stream aluminum is pressed into large bundles called bales and sent to the **reprocessing plant**.

recycled

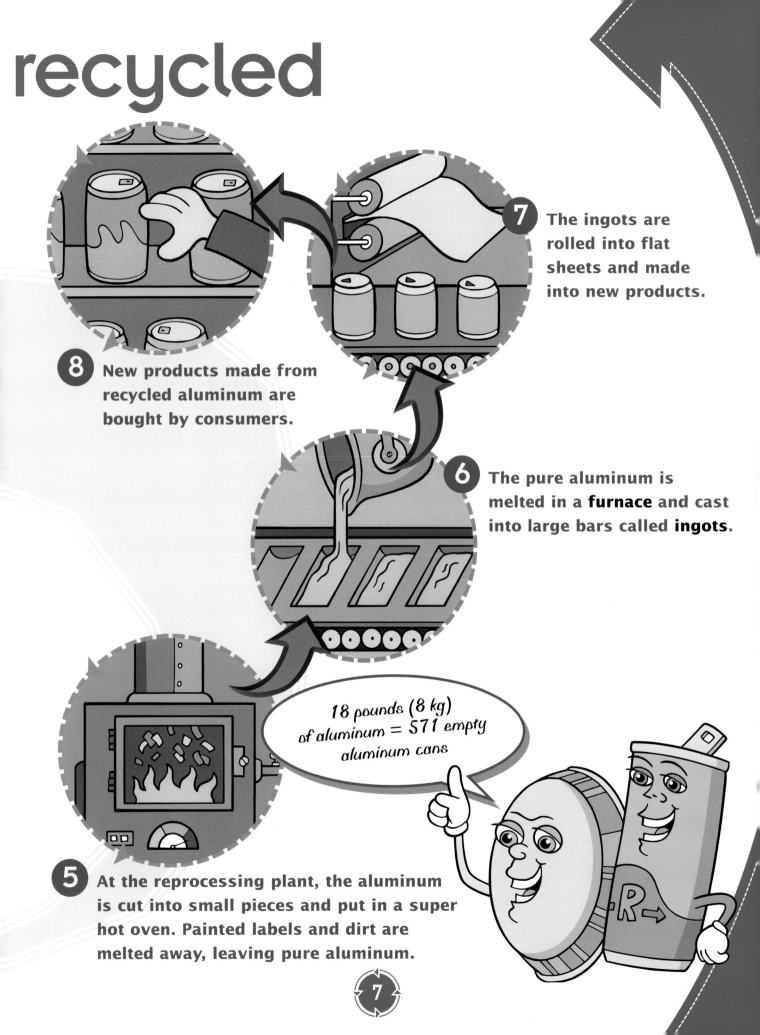

7 The ingots are rolled into flat sheets and made into new products.

8 New products made from recycled aluminum are bought by consumers.

6 The pure aluminum is melted in a **furnace** and cast into large bars called **ingots**.

18 pounds (8 kg) of aluminum = 571 empty aluminum cans

5 At the reprocessing plant, the aluminum is cut into small pieces and put in a super hot oven. Painted labels and dirt are melted away, leaving pure aluminum.

Recycled aluminum

All used aluminum products can be recycled. In fact, most aluminum products are recycled again and again, and never wasted. This is called closed-loop recycling. Some used aluminum, however, is used to make products that are very difficult to recover for recycling. When these products are thrown away, we say the aluminum has been recycled in an open loop.

Closed-loop recycling

Closed-loop recycling happens when used materials are remade into new products again and again. The materials go round in a non-stop loop and are never wasted.

A closed-loop cycle

Closed-loop aluminum products

Products made of different aluminum **alloys** are recycled separately. Some aluminum products that can be recycled in a closed loop are:

🔄 *used drink cans*   These are melted and made into new drink cans.

🔄 *used cooking foil, foil chocolate wrappers, and foil pie plates*   These are recycled to make the same new foil products.

🔄 *high-heat resistant aluminum products, such as used engine parts*   These are recycled into high-heat resistant products again.

🔄 *products made from flat-sheet aluminum, such as used car and aircraft bodies*   These are recycled to make more flat-sheet aluminum products.

New aluminum cans are made from recycled cans.

products

Open-loop recycling

Open-loop recycling happens when materials are made into different products that cannot be recycled again. The materials are reused only once and then thrown away. Many people believe this is not recycling at all because the materials are wasted.

Open-loop aluminum products

Some recycled aluminum is made into products that are usually thrown away and not recycled again. Aluminum products that are usually recycled in an open loop are:

- ↻ *small pieces of foil*   These are too small for recyclers to handle.
- ↻ *aluminum cooking foil and takeout food trays*   These are often **contaminated** with food scraps, so they are not suitable for recycling. Recyclers must store aluminum foil for a long time. Foil contaminated with food attracts ants and other pests, and smells bad.
- ↻ *aluminum foil bonded to cardboard or plastic*   This is often wasted because of the high cost of separating the two materials.

An open-loop cycle

Aluminum bonded to plastic makes metalized film for food packaging, such as chip bags. Aluminum used this way cannot be recovered for recycling.

Why recycle

When used aluminum products are recycled to make new aluminum products:

- ↺ we use fewer of the Earth's natural resources
- ↺ manufacturing is "greener" because recycling creates less pollution than using raw materials
- ↺ we reduce waste, which is better for the environment.

Conserving natural resources

Recycling is an important part of looking after the Earth's natural resources to make sure they are not wasted and do not run out. Natural resources are materials taken from the Earth and used to make products. Aluminum is made from bauxite. Bauxite is found in large deposits in several places in the world. The world has enough bauxite to last for several hundred years, however, it is a **non-renewable** resource. Recycling aluminum causes less damage to the environment than mining bauxite and uses fewer natural resources to generate power for making aluminum.

When aluminum is recycled, plant and animal **habitats** are not disturbed by bauxite mining.

All topsoil and plants are removed at a bauxite strip mine.

How bauxite mining affects the environment

Most bauxite is taken from the ground by strip mining. The topsoil is removed from a strip of land and the bauxite below is dug up and taken away. The topsoil is put back and the next strip of land is mined in the same way. New trees and grasses are planted on the mined strip. It takes many years for plants to grow back, and for birds and animals to return.

Aluminum is made from bauxite.

aluminum?

How aluminum making affects the environment

Making aluminum uses a lot of power, and in most countries this power comes from **hydro-electric power** plants. Hydro-electric power is generated by a steady flow of water turning giant turbines that produce electricity. Large dams are built across rivers to trap the water needed for hydro-electric power plants. Whole river valleys are often flooded by hydro dams, and this creates serious problems for people and the environment.

Hydro dams in South America and Africa have flooded several river valleys, forcing thousands of people to leave their traditional homelands. These people must move to other areas and learn new ways of living and farming. Large areas of plant and animal habitats are destroyed when river valleys are flooded, and disease-carrying mosquitoes breed in the still waters of dams.

The Tucuruí dam, built to supply power for making aluminum, has flooded 1,080 square miles (2,800 sq km) of rain forest in Brazil.

When aluminum is recycled, less hydro-electric power is needed to make new aluminum. Rivers are left to flow naturally, and people and environments are left undisturbed.

"Greener" manufacturing

Recycling is a great way to reduce some of the problems caused when aluminum is manufactured. Aluminum products that are not recycled are made in two steps:

1 Refining: Bauxite is refined from a red rock into a white powder called alumina.

2 Manufacturing: Alumina is **smelted** to make aluminum.

Recycling aluminum is "greener" than manufacturing new aluminum products because fewer raw materials are used and less pollution is created.

How bauxite refining affects the environment

To refine bauxite, it is crushed and mixed in a tank with hot water and a harsh chemical called caustic soda. Caustic soda dissolves the alumina out of the bauxite and leaves all the other materials, iron, clay, and sand, to settle to the bottom of the tank as "red mud." The water containing caustic soda and alumina is piped away from the top of the tank. In modern aluminum plants, the caustic soda is recovered and used again.

Red mud is stored in dams until it dries out. Then it is used to refill old mine sites. In older aluminum plants, however, red mud still contains some caustic soda and must be stored in dams with a thick clay lining. Otherwise the caustic soda can seep into underground water and contaminate rivers and streams.

Recycled aluminum is already refined, so no dangerous caustic soda is used and no red mud is produced.

Red mud is left after alumina is removed from bauxite. Red mud is dried out in dams.

How smelting aluminum affects the environment

At the smelting plant, white alumina powder is dissolved in a "bath" of a hot substance called sodium aluminum fluoride, and a powerful electric current is passed through it. The current makes the alumina separate from the oxygen and other substances, and fall to the bottom as pure aluminum. It is drawn off and cast into ingots. During the smelting process, some fluoride escapes into the air as a gas. Fluorides are highly poisonous substances.

Modern aluminum smelting plants use powerful "scrubbing" systems to remove fluoride gas **emissions**. Small amounts of fluoride still escape into the environment and some scientists believe that even small amounts are dangerous. Very old smelting plants, especially in **developing countries**, release large amounts of fluoride into the air. In Tajikistan, fluoride emissions from an old aluminum smelter are carried by wind into the neighboring country of Uzbekistan. These fluoride emissions have killed food crops and contaminated the meat and milk of farm animals, causing many people to fall ill.

When aluminum is recycled, no dangerous fluoride is released.

All aluminum smelting plants give off some fluoride emissions.

The waste-to-energy plant on the Isle of Man, United Kingdom, will burn 66,140 tons (60,000 t) of waste per year and will supply power to the island's electricity grid.

Reducing waste

Worldwide, 50 percent of all aluminum cans and 25 percent of used aluminum building and transportation materials are thrown away. When aluminum is recycled instead of being thrown away, the amount of waste is reduced and some problems with this waste are solved.

Aluminum in landfills

Landfills are large holes dug in the ground in which waste materials are buried. Aluminum makes up 2.2 percent of the total volume, or amount of space, of all household waste sent to landfills. Aluminum **decomposes**, or breaks down, naturally by absorbing oxygen from the air and **corroding**. Corroding aluminum releases no poisonous substances into landfills. It slowly returns to the soil as aluminum oxide, which is how it started out. However, scientists believe that this process can take hundreds of years.

In some countries, mixed household waste containing aluminum is **incinerated** to generate electricity. Scraps of aluminum foil in household waste give off the same amount of heat as coal when burned. The ash left over from burned aluminum can be safely buried in landfills. Aluminum and aluminum ash buried in landfills cause less harm than some other substances. However, they do take up valuable landfill space and some countries, such as Japan and Switzerland, have no land left to use as landfills.

Aluminum litter

Some people get rid of their aluminum waste by throwing it away as litter. When aluminum cans are dumped as litter they can cause problems. In hot, wet, tropical climates, millions of discarded cans fill with water and become breeding grounds for mosquitoes. Tropical mosquitoes carry dangerous diseases that kill thousands of people every year. Aluminum cans dropped on the ground also endanger small animals, such as lizards. They crawl inside and starve when they cannot get out.

Aluminum releases no poisonous substances as it corrodes, however, it does decompose into fine metal particles, just as iron does when it rusts. If rainwater washes these particles into lakes, rivers, and streams, they can clog the gills of fish and make it difficult for them to breathe.
Fish that eat aluminum particles may die from absorbing the metal.

Mosquitoes breeding inside discarded cans or jars spread deadly diseases, such as malaria.

When aluminum is recycled instead of being thrown away as litter, the lives of people and wildlife are less at risk.

For and against

Question:
Can the Earth sustain its growing population?

Answer:
Yes, if people act now to preserve the environment and manage the Earth's resources better.

Question:
Can this be achieved just by recycling?

"YES" The "yes" case for recycling

✔ Recycling aluminum conserves bauxite, a non-renewable resource.

✔ When aluminum is recycled, there is less bauxite mining and less need to build hydro dams. This means large areas of plant and animal habitats are left undisturbed.

✔ Recycling aluminum reduces caustic soda use and fluoride emissions, which are both dangerous pollutants.

✔ When aluminum is recycled, less landfill space is needed.

✔ Aluminum recycling removes dangerous litter from the environment, where it can kill or injure people and wildlife.

✔ Lightweight aluminum is cheap to transport. Collecting it for recycling does not use up large amounts of scarce **fossil fuels**.

> Aluminum weighs far less than paper, steel, or glass.

Aluminum is a valuable metal. Many charities and community groups raise money by collecting aluminum cans and selling them to recyclers.

recycling

Question:
Do most people agree that recycling is a good idea?

Answer:
Yes.

Question:
Will recycling fix all the problems caused by aluminum manufacturing and aluminum waste?

"NO" The "no" case against recycling

✗ Some aluminum products are not recycled because they are made of mixed materials, which are too expensive to separate, such as steel cans with aluminum bases and lids.

✗ Harmful substances are released into the atmosphere when aluminum cans are "baked" to remove their outer coatings.

✗ Different aluminum products cannot be recycled together. They must be collected and recycled separately because they contain different alloys.

✗ Aluminum foil is difficult to recycle because it is collected in very small quantities and is often contaminated with food.

It is better for the environment to throw away very greasy cooking foil than to use a lot of hot water and detergent trying to get it clean.

✗ Recycled aluminum is easily contaminated by liquids inside cans that turn to steam during reprocessing, by plastics and paper that burn and create hot spots, and by small amounts of other metals that weaken aluminum.

Reduce, reuse,

Recycling is a great idea, but it is just one answer to the problems of how to conserve resources, reduce manufacturing pollution and waste, and protect the environment. There are other things we can do that are even better than recycling. We can reduce, reuse, and rethink what we use.

Reduce

The best and quickest way to reduce aluminum waste is to use less aluminum! Reducing is easy. Some of the ways you can reduce aluminum use are to:

- buy fewer disposable aluminum products, such as throw-away drink cans. Buy drinks in larger containers, or better still, mix up drinks at home

- use less aluminum cooking foil and fewer food trays when preparing food

- buy wooden window and door frames instead of aluminum window and door frames

- stop buying aluminum products that are not easily recycled, or are not being recycled in your area. These may include aluminum-lined drink packs, and chip bags made of metalized plastic film

- write, telephone, or e-mail the manufacturers of these products and tell them you have stopped buying them and state the reason why.

Many people replace old aluminum window frames with wooden ones. Wooden window frames look attractive and can be bought second-hand from building material recyclers.

rethink

Aircraft contain a lot of aluminum. Used aircraft are stripped and the spare parts used for other airplanes. Old aircraft shells are given to firefighting training schools, and some are made into homes, restaurants, or tourist offices.

Reuse

Some aluminum products can be used again and again instead of being thrown away. Some of the ways that aluminum products can be reused are:

- cooking foil and food trays that are not too greasy can be washed clean and used again
- unwanted aluminum cookware can be given away to charity stores for someone else to use
- aluminum outdoor furniture and car parts can be sold or bought second-hand.

Rethink

Everyone can come up with new ideas. Some new ideas for changing the way we use aluminum products and materials are:

- governments can put a deposit tax on aluminum cans, which is paid back when cans are returned. This encourages more people to return cans for recycling
- industries can recycle aluminum more easily and cheaply by developing products made from mixed alloys
- manufacturers can find other ways to make products look attractive without using metalized plastic and aluminum-coated paper.

Governments around the world are helping and encouraging people to recycle more aluminum.

Running a recycling program

Recycle

In Uruguay, South America, young volunteers collect aluminum cans for recycling as part of a program called Prolata. The program was started in Montevideo, a city famous for its white sandy beaches. Thousands of tourists visited the beaches every year, but left them littered with aluminum cans. The local government of Montevideo helped start Prolata by setting up 200 bright blue aluminum recycling bins, not only along the beaches, but also throughout the city. The volunteers' first job was to hand out pamphlets to tourists, asking them to deposit their cans in the bins.

Uruguay has no aluminum industry. All cans collected have to be washed, crushed, and stored until 22 tons (20 t) are collected. The cans are then sold to an aluminum smelting plant in the neighboring country of Brazil. Today, there are more than 600 blue recycling bins throughout Uruguay, and they are emptied regularly by Prolata volunteers. The money raised is used to send young people to school who could not afford to go otherwise.

Uruguay is famous for its beautiful beaches. The Prolata program was started to keep the beaches clean.

GOVERNMENT APPROVED

Sweden is a very small country with little space for landfills. Recycling aluminum stops it from going to landfills.

Passing recycling laws

GOVERNMENT APPROVED

Sweden is one of the smallest countries in Europe, and it has the highest aluminum recycling rate of any country in the world. Back in 1982, the Swedish government saw that aluminum cans were going to take up valuable landfill space, and create serious litter problems. The government decided that at least 75 percent of all aluminum cans had to be recycled, otherwise all aluminum cans would be banned. The government passed its first aluminum recycling law in 1984 by putting a deposit tax of 25 öre (about 3¢) on each can. When people returned the cans, the tax was given back to them. This encouraged people to return the cans for recycling.

When only 65 percent of cans were returned, the government passed a second law raising the deposit tax to 50 öre (about 7¢) per can. The new deposit worked. The recycling rate reached 75 percent. Today, Sweden's recycling rate for aluminum cans is more than 90 percent. The average recycling rate for all other countries in Europe is only 40 percent.

Industries are developing new ways to reduce, recycle, and rethink the way aluminum is collected.

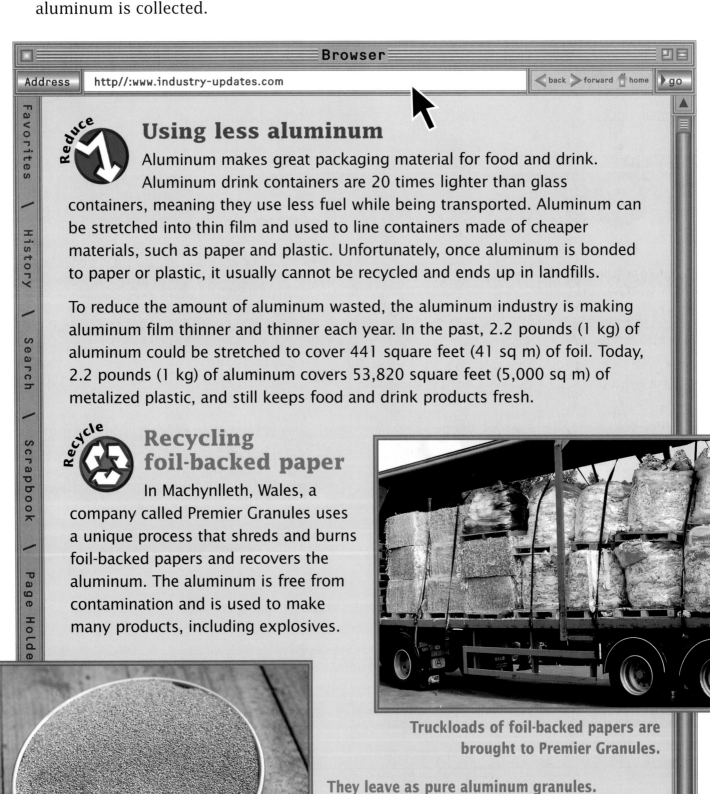

Browser

Address http//:www.industry-updates.com

back forward home go

Favorites \ History \ Search \ Scrapbook \ Page Holde

Reduce

Using less aluminum

Aluminum makes great packaging material for food and drink. Aluminum drink containers are 20 times lighter than glass containers, meaning they use less fuel while being transported. Aluminum can be stretched into thin film and used to line containers made of cheaper materials, such as paper and plastic. Unfortunately, once aluminum is bonded to paper or plastic, it usually cannot be recycled and ends up in landfills.

To reduce the amount of aluminum wasted, the aluminum industry is making aluminum film thinner and thinner each year. In the past, 2.2 pounds (1 kg) of aluminum could be stretched to cover 441 square feet (41 sq m) of foil. Today, 2.2 pounds (1 kg) of aluminum covers 53,820 square feet (5,000 sq m) of metalized plastic, and still keeps food and drink products fresh.

Recycle

Recycling foil-backed paper

In Machynlleth, Wales, a company called Premier Granules uses a unique process that shreds and burns foil-backed papers and recovers the aluminum. The aluminum is free from contamination and is used to make many products, including explosives.

Truckloads of foil-backed papers are brought to Premier Granules.

They leave as pure aluminum granules.

22

doing

Address   http//:www.industry-updates.com   ▶ go

 Recycle   **Rethink**

Reverse vending machines

More countries are putting a deposit tax on aluminum drink cans to encourage people to return them for recycling. The deposit is paid when the can is bought, and given back to the customer when the can is returned to the store. To make it easy for customers and store owners to take back used cans, industry has developed reverse vending machines.

The machines are simple. The customer feeds the empty can into a slot. The machine reads the bar code on the can and pays out the correct deposit for that can. The machine squashes the can flat and drops it in a storage bin. When the reverse vending machine is ready to be emptied, the whole storage bin can be removed and an empty bin is put in its place.

A reverse vending machine takes used aluminum cans back for recycling.

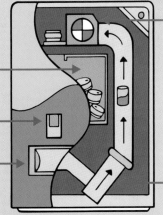

3 Cans are squashed flat

4 Cans fall into a storage bin

5 Coins come out the deposit slot

1 Cans go in the slot

2 Air pushes can up a pipe

How a reverse vending machine works

What communities

People working together in communities are proving that a lot more can be done to recycle aluminum.

Thursday July 3

Your local newspaper

THE DAILY HERALD

Morning edition

Scouts help with recycling

In the rural community of Oakville, Australia, scouts and their families are regular aluminum recyclers. All year round they save aluminum cans: at school, work, and home. Anyone who holds a party in the area is given a couple of horse feedbags in which to toss empty cans.

Once a year the scouts hold an aluminum recycling drive. Cubs, scouts, venturers, and their families join the Clean Up Australia campaign, held one Sunday in March. Groups set off along the roads, picking up all the litter they find. It is brought to the scout hall, and the aluminum cans are separated from the rest of the garbage.

Oakville scouts collect aluminum for recycling on Clean Up Australia day.

Scouts also act as can crushers, stomping on them to squash them flat. The council garbage truck takes away the mixed garbage, and the scouts take the aluminum cans to a recycler. The money raised is used to send scouts to the Australian Jamboree, held once every three years.

...ewspaper

Recycle

Working together

In Fraserburgh, Scotland, a group of five people with disabilities started a recycling business. They wanted to help the environment and also create jobs for themselves. The group decided to collect aluminum cans for recycling. Others in the community helped them get started. The local Aberdeenshire Council gave them a workshop space and a small van. The Aluminum Can Recycling Association printed advertising leaflets for them, and gave them collection bags. The group called their recycling business Can-Do, and handed out leaflets to local stores and hotels.

Twenty-five businesses agreed to take a collection bag and fill it with cans.

In the first year, Can-Do collected 1.7 tons (1.5 t) of aluminum cans. They used a homemade crushing machine to squash the cans flat. Today, Can-Do employs 22 people and collects 24 tons (22 t) of aluminum cans and foil each year from 200 hotels, stores, factories, offices, and schools. They have a large truck and special machines to flatten cans and press them into bales. In 2002, Can-Do won the Best Community Project prize in the National Recycling Awards.

Can-Do workers use a can crushing-machine to flatten cans for recycling.

What individuals are

Individuals are inspiring others to recycle and reuse more aluminum, often in creative ways.

Individuals making your planet a better place.

Green Fingers Newsletter

Reuse ›››

Making aluminum art

Linda and Opie O'Brien began creating sculptures from used materials after they moved to Lake Erie in Ohio. While walking along the lake shore, the O'Briens found interesting objects that other people had thrown away. They brought these "found objects" back to their art workshop, called Burnt Offerings Studio. The O'Briens started to use these "found objects" in their sculptures. One day they built a sculpture entirely from reused materials.

The O'Briens like working with aluminum. It catches people's attention because it looks big and heavy, but aluminum is really very light and easy to work with. The O'Briens fix their sculptures together using screws, nuts, bolts, rivets, and wire. The base for each sculpture is a brick, also found by the lake. The O'Briens like to work with recycled materials and "found objects." They believe that every piece is special and has a story to tell.

"Dr. Recyclabotto," by Linda and Opie O'Brien, is made from 100 percent reused materials. The arms and legs come from an aluminum baby carriage found by the lake.

doing

Sue and Graham Gooderham are award-winning recyclers.

Recycling aluminum cans and foil

In 1996, Sue and Graham Gooderham started collecting used aluminum to help raise money for the Evesham Methodist Church in England. They placed a box in the church parking lot where people could leave cans and foil. Every few days the Gooderhams brought the aluminum home and sorted it in their garage. They squashed the cans flat and stored them in bags, and bagged the foil separately. When a large enough load was ready, they took it to be recycled. Local businesses and clubs began saving cans for the Gooderhams as well.

Even their granddaughter collected lunch foil from her friends at school. She saved it for her "aluminum grandad" to recycle.

In 2002, Sue and Graham's recycling efforts saw their church win the national Eco-Congregation Award. The award is given every year to a church involved in a project that helps the environment. During that year, the Gooderhams recycled more than 78,000 cans and 100 bags of foil. The money was raised to help restore the Evesham Methodist Church, which is almost 100 years old.

What you can do

You can do all sorts of activities to help recycle, reduce, and reuse aluminum. You can also get others interested and come up with ideas to stop aluminum from harming the environment. Make a weekly "Aluminum 3-R scorecard" for yourself or your class.

What to do:

1 Draw up a scorecard with headings like the one shown below.
2 Write down each time you or your class do something to recycle, reduce, or reuse aluminum.
3 Reward yourself or your class with a green star for each activity that you do.

Aluminum 3-R scorecard

Recycle	Reduce	Reuse	Get others interested	Other things
Washed our drink cans and put them in the recycling bin.	Mixed our own drinks for a Sunday picnic. Bought ZERO cans!	Cut scraps of used aluminum foil into circles for my "Sun and Planets" project.	Talked to our scout troop about saving cans-for-cash!	Kim and I picked up cans that were littering the park.
Made one ball of all the foil from our Easter eggs and recycled it.	Will not buy shiny foil-backed wrapping paper this Christmas because the aluminum cannot be recycled.	Strung aluminum yogurt tops across the strawberry patch to keep the birds away.	Talked to Uncle Peshar about saving his aluminum cans for our scout troop.	
	Voted for wooden outdoor furniture instead of aluminum. We got wooden furniture!!!		Gave a talk to the class about aluminum products that CANNOT be recycled.	
★★★	★★★	★★★	★★★	★

Get others interested

You can make a poster or leaflets to show other people how to recycle aluminum. Most people want to recycle their aluminum waste but are not sure how.

A bold heading will catch people's attention.

State which aluminum products can be recycled from home.

ALUMINUM RECYCLING

WHAT CAN BE RECYCLED FROM HOME?

YES
- ✓ drink cans
- ✓ aerosol cans
- ✓ food trays
- ✓ cooking foil
- ✓ chocolate foil wrapping

NO
- ✗ foil-backed paper
- ✗ metalized plastics
- ✗ cookware
- ✗ car parts
- ✗ garden furniture
- ✗ door and window frames

State the types of aluminum products that cannot be recycled from home.

HOW TO RECYCLE:

Cleaning avoids attracting ants and other pests.

1 Rinse cans clean and squash flat.

2 Empty out aerosol cans. Do NOT flatten.

3 Remove food and oil from foil without using too much water.

4 Roll foil into a ball or tube.

 Thank you for recycling.

Take damaged goods to scrap metal dealers. Give undamaged goods to charity shops or sell them at yard sales.

Foil is stored for months before reprocessing. Food contamination makes it smell.

Flattened cans take up less room.

Add interest to your leaflets with pictures or computer clip art images.

Decomposition timeline

This timeline shows how long it takes for products and materials to break down and return to the soil when left exposed to air and sunlight.

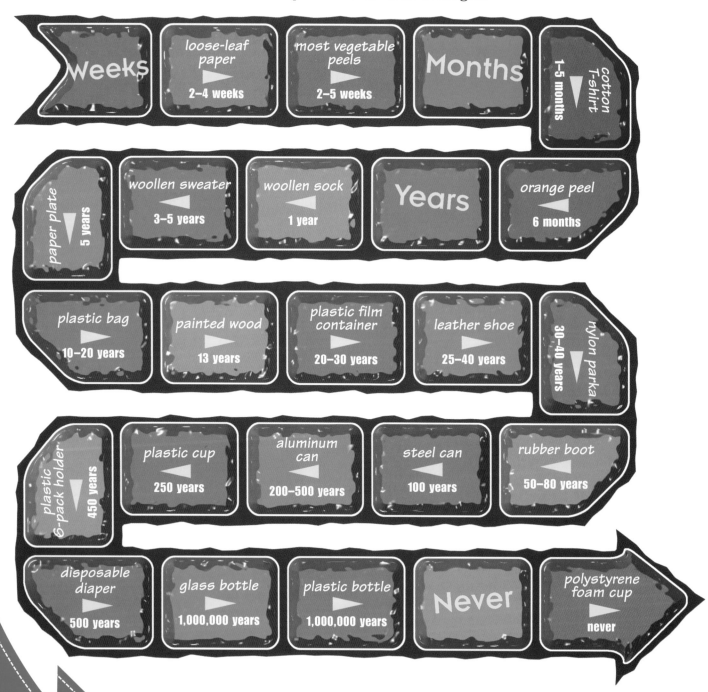

Weeks

loose-leaf paper
2–4 weeks

most vegetable peels
2–5 weeks

Months

cotton T-shirt
1–5 months

paper plate
5 years

woollen sweater
3–5 years

woollen sock
1 year

Years

orange peel
6 months

plastic bag
10–20 years

painted wood
13 years

plastic film container
20–30 years

leather shoe
25–40 years

nylon parka
30–40 years

plastic 6-pack holder
450 years

plastic cup
250 years

aluminum can
200–500 years

steel can
100 years

rubber boot
50–80 years

disposable diaper
500 years

glass bottle
1,000,000 years

plastic bottle
1,000,000 years

Never

polystyrene foam cup
never

Glossary

alloys mixes of different metals

alumina a mixture of aluminum and oxygen

bauxite a red rock made of aluminum, oxygen, iron, and clay

contaminated ruined by harmful material, such as aluminum foil ruined by food scraps

corroding wearing away by a chemical reaction, such as aluminum crumbling away after it has absorbed oxygen

decomposes breaks down into simple substances through the activity of tiny living organisms called bacteria

developed countries countries where most people have good living conditions and use a lot of manufactured products

developing countries countries where most people have poor living conditions and cannot afford to use a lot of manufactured products

emissions gases or small particles released into the atmosphere, such as fluoride gas released during aluminum smelting

fossil fuels fuels, such as petroleum, coal, and natural gas, which formed from the remains of ancient plants and animals

furnace a very hot oven used to melt materials, such as aluminum

habitats areas where particular plants and animals live and breed

hydro-electric power electric power produced by a strong flow of water

incinerated burned in a closed container called an incinerator

ingots large bars of metal, such as aluminum

landfills large holes in the ground in which waste materials are buried

natural resources materials taken from the Earth and used to make products, such as bauxite used to make aluminum

non-renewable cannot be made or grown again

pollution dirty or harmful waste material that damages air, water, or land

pure streams lots of aluminum items of the same type, either foil or cans

raw materials materials that have not been processed or treated before, such as bauxite mined from the ground

refining purifying or improving the quality of a raw material, such as bauxite, taken from the Earth

reprocessing plant a factory where used aluminum is made into new aluminum products

smelted melted alumina to separate out and remove the aluminum it contains

Index

A

aircraft 5, 8, 19
alumina 5, 12–13
aluminum alloys 8, 17, 19
aluminum furniture 5, 19, 28, 29
aluminum ingots 7, 13
animals 10, 11, 13, 15, 16

B

bauxite 5, 10, 12, 16
bauxite mining 10, 16
building materials 5, 18, 29
burning aluminum 14, 22

C

car parts 5, 8, 19, 29
closed-loop recycling 8
communities 4, 16, 24–25
conservation 10, 16, 18

D

decomposition 14, 15, 30
deposit tax 19, 21, 23

E

environment 4, 10, 11, 12–13, 15, 18, 25, 27, 28

F

farming 11, 13
fluoride emissions 13, 16
fossil fuels 16

G

governments 4, 19, 20, 21
"greener" manufacturing 4, 10, 12–13

H

habitats 10, 11, 16
history of aluminum 5
hydro dams 11, 16
hydro-electric power 11

I

individuals 4, 26–27
industries 4, 19, 22–23

L

landfills 6, 14, 16, 21, 22
laws 21
litter 15, 16, 21, 24, 28

N

natural resources 4, 10
non-renewable resources 10, 16

O

open-loop recycling 9

P

plants 10, 11, 16
pollution 4, 10, 13, 16
population growth 4
power use 10, 11

R

raw materials 4, 10, 12
recycling cans 6, 8, 16, 17, 19, 20, 21, 23, 24, 25, 27, 28, 29
recycling foil 6, 8–9, 17, 22, 25, 27, 28, 29
reducing 4, 14, 18, 22, 28
reprocessing 6–7, 17, 29
rethinking 4, 18–19, 23
reusing 4, 18–19, 26, 28
reverse vending machines 23

S

schools 20, 24, 27
scrap metal 6, 29
smelting 12, 13, 20
smelting plant 13, 20

W

waste 4, 9, 10, 14, 17, 18, 22, 29
waste reduction 4, 10, 14, 18, 22
water contamination 12, 15
water use 11
wildlife 15, 16